CW01663656

ESTELLE MUTUM

Empower Your Mind: 30 Days of Affirmations for Women

Unlock the Power of Positive Thinking Through Affirmations

GIRL POWER ROCKS PUBLISHING

First published by Girl Power Rocks Publishing 2024

Copyright © 2024 by Estelle Mutum

All rights reserved. No part of this publication may be reproduced, stored or transmitted in any form or by any means, electronic, mechanical, photocopying, recording, scanning, or otherwise without written permission from the publisher. It is illegal to copy this book, post it to a website, or distribute it by any other means without permission.

Estelle Mutum asserts the moral right to be identified as the author of this work.

Estelle Mutum has no responsibility for the persistence or accuracy of URLs for external or third-party Internet Websites referred to in this publication and does not guarantee that any content on such Websites is, or will remain, accurate or appropriate.

Designations used by companies to distinguish their products are often claimed as trademarks. All brand names and product names used in this book and on its cover are trade names, service marks, trademarks and registered trademarks of their respective owners. The publishers and the book are not associated with any product or vendor mentioned in this book. None of the companies referenced within the book have endorsed the book.

First edition

This book was professionally typeset on Reedsy.
Find out more at reedsy.com

To the Girl Power Rocks Community.
You ROCK!

Contents

Foreword

An Ode to Affirmations

In the theatre of the mind, where thoughts dance and sway,
Let affirmations be the light that brightens your play.
Repeat with me through the day's rise and decline,
"I hold the power to change; this life is mine."

"I am enough," let these words ring true,
A simple phrase, a powerful cue.
With each utterance, let self-doubt unwind.
Unleash the strength that's in your mind.

"I choose to grow," say it with zeal,
In every moment, let this be your seal.
Plant seeds of progress in your mental terrain,
Nourish with hope; let positivity reign.

"I will succeed," let this anthem soar,
As you echo these words, watch your spirit roar.
Crafting visions in your mind's own shrine,
Painting your future with a brush divine.

In whispers or shouts, let ***"I am loved"*** take flight,
Feel the warmth, let it banish the night.

An affirmation, a heart's resounding chime,
Bringing peace and joy, transcending time.

With each new dawn, ***"I am brave"*** resounds,
Across mind's horizons, beyond bounds.
Face the unknown, let courage be your guide,
On the winds of boldness, you will ride.

"Today, I thrive," let it be your creed,
In the garden of thought, let this be the seed.
From morning's first light to the evening's soft hum,
With affirmations, into your power, you'll come.

So let these words a steadfast friend be,
A chorus of empowerment, a mind's jubilee.
With each affirmation, a step toward divine,
In the heart's quiet chambers, watch yourself shine.

Written Especially For You

Estelle Mutum

Founder, Girl Power Rocks

xxx

Empower Your Mind With Affirmations

Welcome to "Empower Your Mind: 30 Days of Affirmations for Women"

Girl Power Rocks Self-Empowerment

Welcome to the Girl Power Rocks Book Series, where our focus is on Unleashing your Girl Power! By supporting you with differing empowering tools to help you on your journey of self-empowerment. This guide takes you on an empowering journey of Affirmations.

Affirmations are positive, specific statements that can help you to overcome self-sabotage, negative thoughts and limiting beliefs. When you repeatedly affirm positivity to yourself, you start by laying the groundwork for lasting change.

This book harnesses that power, providing you with a daily dose of affirmation for the next 30 days to guide you towards a more confident, self-empowered YOU!

The History of Affirmations

Affirmations have a long and rich history, dating back centuries as part of various spiritual and religious practices around the world.

The concept involves using positive, repetitive statements designed to encourage a positive mindset and self-belief, influencing both conscious and subconscious thoughts.

The modern use of affirmations became more widely recognised with the New Thought movement in the late 19th and early 20th centuries, which embraced the idea that positive thinking could influence personal outcomes. Figures like Norman Vincent Peale further popularised this with his 1952 book, "The Power of Positive Thinking," and Louise Hay, in the 1980s, championed affirmations as a tool for emotional and physical healing. Today, affirmations are used globally for personal development, mental health, and wellness, reflecting their enduring appeal and the universal desire for positive transformation.

The Science of Affirmations

Affirmations are more than just feel-good quotes or motivational phrases; they are supported by a growing body of scientific research that highlights their effectiveness in various mental and emotional health aspects. Studies have shown that engaging in positive self-affirmations activates regions of the brain associated with self-related processing and the valuation of important aspects of the self.

This neurological activity can enhance emotional resilience and a more positive outlook. Furthermore, affirmations have been found to reduce stress, increase problem-solving abilities under pressure, and improve overall performance in challenging situations. The practice of affirmations can help individuals combat negative thoughts and reinforce their sense of self-worth and personal integrity, making them a powerful tool for personal development and emotional well-being.

How to Use This Guide

To reap the full benefits of "Empower Your Mind," integrate these affirmations into your daily routine. Each morning or evening, find a quiet space where you can sit comfortably and reflect.

- Read the day's affirmation aloud, clearly and confidently.
- Repeat it three times, each with more conviction than the last.
- Visualise the words sinking into your consciousness, planting seeds of change.
- Carry the day's affirmation with you, make it visible, letting its resonance uplift you at moments of uncertainty or challenge.

The Journaling Experience

Accompanying these affirmations, we encourage you to keep a journal. A journal is a great way for you to express your thoughts and feelings freely and notice any shifts you may encounter as you progress through the 30 days.

Journaling is a powerful tool for self-reflection. It's a safe space (please don't share it; this is personal to you!). It will allow you to explore the experience of Affirmations deeper and record your experiences during that time. It will also help you track progress, celebrate, and learn from your challenges. There is something quite magical about journaling and getting something written out of your head and written down on a page in front of you. This activity in itself is both a mental and visual affirmation.

Are you ready to start your Self-Empowerment Journey?

As you turn to Day 1, enter with an open heart and a mind ready for growth. Remember, this is your path to tread, your mind to empower, and your life to celebrate. Let's begin.

Day 1

Affirmation: "I am worthy of respect and love."

Today's Focus:

Today, we begin our journey with a foundational truth that's essential to embrace: You are worthy of respect and love. In a world that often demands we earn our worth, it's crucial to remember that your value isn't contingent on your accomplishments, appearances, or others' opinions. This affirmation is about recognising your intrinsic worth and treating yourself with the kindness and respect you deserve.

Reflection Question:

Reflect on moments when you felt respected and loved. What qualities were you embodying, or actions were you taking that made you feel most valued? Conversely, consider times when you haven't felt worthy of respect and love. What beliefs or circumstances contributed to those feelings? Understanding these contrasts can illuminate the path to nurturing your self-worth.

Action Step:

To integrate today's affirmation into your life, start by writing three qualities you love about yourself in your journal. These can be aspects of your character, achievements you're proud of, or simply parts of your personality that bring you joy. Next, perform an act of kindness for yourself. It could be as simple as allowing yourself a few moments of quiet with a cup of tea, taking a short walk in nature, or indulging in your favourite treat. This act is a practice of showing yourself love and respect.

Today's Notes:

Here, you will find each day a space to jot down your thoughts and reflections on the day's affirmation, insights from the reflection question, and any feelings or discoveries that arose from the action step.

Words of Wisdom:

Day 1: Embrace your worthiness of love and respect today and every day. You are deserving, you are valued, and you are loved just as you are.

Day 1 Girl Power Notes

Your very own space for notes!

Day 2

Affirmation: "I have the power to change my story."

Today's Focus:

Today, we delve into the profound truth that your past does not define your future. Every moment presents an opportunity to write a new chapter in your life story. This affirmation, "I have the power to change my story," is about recognising and embracing your ability to influence the direction of your life. It's about moving from a place of feeling stuck to a position of empowerment and action. You're not just a character in your story; you are your very own author and CEO of YOU INC!

Reflection Question:

Reflect on an aspect of your life you've felt was out of your control or predetermined. How does acknowledging your power to change your narrative alter your feelings about this aspect? Consider how the realisation of your autonomy, your girl power, can inspire a different approach or mindset towards this part of your life.

Action Step:

Identify one small but significant change you can make today that reflects the new chapter you wish to write for yourself; this could be as simple as dedicating 15 minutes to a hobby you've neglected or as bold as making a career-related decision you've been postponing. Write this action down, and more importantly, commit to doing it. Remember, change doesn't have to be monumental to be meaningful. Small steps often lead to significant shifts.

Today's Notes:

Take a moment to jot down your thoughts or feelings about today's affirmation. How does the idea of changing your story resonate with you? Are there fears or doubts that arise when you think about taking control of your narrative(the story you tell yourself)? Writing these down can help you acknowledge and address them as you move forward.

Words of Wisdom:

Day 2: Your Story is yours to write. Grab your pen with confidence, and let today be the day you start a new and empowering chapter.

Day 2 Girl Power Notes

Your very own space for notes!

Day 3

Affirmation: "I am deserving of love and kindness from myself and others."

Today's Focus:

We explore the foundation of self-love and the importance of recognising your inherent worth. This affirmation, "I am deserving of love and kindness from myself and others," invites you to reflect on how you treat yourself and how you allow others to treat you. It's about understanding that deserving love isn't contingent on meeting certain conditions or expectations; it's a birthright.

Reflection Question:

Think about the ways you show love and kindness to yourself. Are there areas where you could be more compassionate or supportive? Similarly, consider the quality of love and kindness you accept from others. Are there relationships in your life where these qualities are lacking, and how does that affect your self-esteem?

Action Step:

Today, commit to one act of self-love and one act of setting boundaries where you demand love and respect from others. For self-love, it might be treating yourself to a favourite meal, taking a long bath, or simply allowing yourself an hour of guilt-free relaxation. Setting boundaries could involve saying 'NO' to an unreasonable request or expressing a need in a relationship. These actions reinforce the message that you are worthy of love and kindness in all aspects of your life.

Today's Notes:

Document your chosen acts of self-love and boundary-setting. How did it feel to consciously decide to treat yourself with kindness? Were there any challenges in setting boundaries, and how did you overcome them? Reflecting on these experiences can deepen your understanding of your self-worth and how it's expressed in your daily life.

Words of Wisdom:

Day 3: Today, recognise your worth and allow yourself to receive love and kindness. Believe in your heart.

Day 3 Girl Power Notes

Your very own space for notes!

Day 4

Affirmation: "I am a beacon of love and positivity."

Today's Focus:

In today's affirmation, we embrace the powerful role of love and positivity in our lives. By declaring, ***"I am a beacon of love and positivity,"*** you acknowledge your capacity to positively influence your environment and the people around you. This affirmation is about recognising the strength of your emotional presence and the ripple effect of your attitudes and actions. It's a call to embody love and positivity, not just for others but also for yourself.

Reflection Question:

Reflect on how expressing love and positivity changes your interactions and feelings throughout the day. Can you recall a moment when someone else's positivity significantly impacted you? How can you embody that same positive energy to uplift yourself and those around you, and how can you distance yourself from negative people who impact your positive energy?

Action Step:

Today, commit to performing at least one act of kindness or positivity. It could be something as simple as sharing a genuine compliment, offering help without being asked, or sending a thoughtful message to a friend or family member. Notice how this act of positivity makes you feel and how it affects the person on the receiving end.

Today's Notes:

After completing your act of kindness, take a few moments to write about the experience. How did it feel to be a source of positivity? Did you notice any changes in your mood or outlook? Reflecting on these questions will help you understand the impact of love and positivity on your life and those around you.

Words of Wisdom:

Day 4: Your light is infectious, and your love is profound. Shine brightly today and watch the world light up around you.

Day 4 Girl Power Notes

Your very own space for notes!

Day 5

Affirmation: "My challenges lead to growth."

Today's Focus:

Today, we shift our perspective on challenges and obstacles. By affirming, ***"My challenges lead to growth,"*** we recognise that every difficulty we encounter is an opportunity to learn, develop resilience, and become stronger. This affirmation encourages you to view challenges not as insurmountable barriers but as stepping stones to personal evolution and empowerment. It's about embracing the journey, including its ups and downs, with an open heart and a growth mindset.

Reflection Question:

Think about a challenge you recently faced or are currently facing. How has it pushed you to grow or change in ways you might not have anticipated? What strengths have you discovered in yourself as a result?

Action Step:

Identify a challenge you're currently experiencing and outline one positive action you can take to address it. This action should not only aim at overcoming the challenge but also at personal growth. Whether it's seeking out new knowledge, asking for help, or simply adjusting your attitude, choose a step that moves you forward.

Today's Notes:

Write down the challenge you're focusing on and the action step you've identified. Reflect on how framing this challenge as an opportunity for growth changes your feelings towards it. Are you more motivated to tackle it? Do you feel more capable or empowered? Noting these reflections can help solidify your growth mindset.

Words of Wisdom:

Day 5: Look at today's challenge as shaping yourself into the remarkable person you are becoming.

Day 5 Girl Power Notes

Your very own space for notes!

Day 6

Affirmation: "I celebrate my unique journey and where it's leading me."

Today's Focus:

Today's affirmation encourages you to embrace and celebrate your unique path, including all its twists, turns, and milestones. "***I celebrate my unique journey and where it's leading me***" is about acknowledging that your life is uniquely yours, with its own set of challenges, victories, and lessons. This affirmation invites you to appreciate your progress and trust in the direction you're heading, even if the destination isn't always clear.

Reflection Question:

Reflect on the milestones and significant moments that have shaped your journey so far. How have these experiences contributed to who you are today? How does celebrating your journey shift your perspective on current challenges or goals?

Action Step:

Create a visual representation of your journey; this could be a simple timeline, a collage, or a vision board that includes past milestones, present realities, and future aspirations. Place it somewhere you can see daily as a reminder to celebrate your unique path and the growth it brings.

Today's Notes:

After creating your visual representation, take a moment to write about the experience. Which aspects of your journey are you most proud of? How does visualising your journey enhance your appreciation for it and inspire confidence in where you're headed? Reflecting on these questions can deepen your connection to your personal narrative and its value.

Words of Wisdom:

Day 6: Your path is yours alone! Rich, distinctive and worthy of celebration. Take a moment today to honour your personal journey.

Day 6 Girl Power Notes

Your very own space for notes!

Day 7

Affirmation: "I allow myself to be who I truly am."

Today's Focus:

This affirmation invites you to embrace and express your authentic self, free from the expectations and judgments of others. "***I allow myself to be who I truly am***" is about giving yourself permission to live truthfully and fully, honouring your desires, beliefs, and feelings. It's a commitment to authenticity, recognising that your true self is your greatest strength.

Reflection Question:

Think about moments when you felt you couldn't fully express yourself. What held you back? How does it feel to imagine a life where you allow yourself to be authentically you without fear of judgement?

Action Step:

Choose one small but significant way to express your true self today. It could be wearing something that feels very 'you,' sharing an opinion you've held back, or engaging in an activity that brings you joy but you've avoided out of concern for what others might think. Notice how it feels to take this step towards authenticity.

Today's Notes:

Write about the action you chose and your experience taking it. How did it feel to express your authentic self? Were there any surprises in how you felt or how others reacted? Reflecting on this can help reinforce the value of authenticity in your life.

Words of Wisdom:

Day 7: Unveil your true self to the world today. Be your authentic self.

Day 7 Girl Power Notes

Your very own space for notes!

Day 8

Affirmation: "I embrace change as an opportunity for growth."

Today's Focus:

Change often comes with uncertainty, but it also brings new opportunities for growth and learning. This affirmation encourages you to view change positively as a catalyst for personal development and new experiences. Embracing change means stepping out of your comfort zone and trusting in your ability to adapt and thrive.

Reflection Question:

Think about a time when a change led to unexpected growth or a positive outcome. How did the experience change your perspective on new beginnings or transitions?

Action Step:

Identify one change you've been resisting and list the potential growth opportunities it offers. Commit to one actionable step you can take to embrace this change more openly.

Today's Notes:

Reflect on your feelings about change and how they might evolve by viewing change as an opportunity. Note any apprehensions you have and how you might address them.

Words of Wisdom:

Day 8: Open your arms to change and let it shape you. Each new twist and turn is a path to growth, a learning experience, for you to embrace.

Day 8 Girl Power Notes

Your very own space for notes!

Day 9

Affirmation: "I am worthy of love and kindness from myself and others."

Today's Focus:

This affirmation centres on self-love and the acceptance of kindness from others. It's a reminder that you are deserving of love and kindness, not just from the people around you but from yourself as well. Practising self-compassion and allowing yourself to receive love from others are crucial steps towards building self-esteem.

Reflection Question:

How do you show love and kindness to yourself? Are there barriers that make it difficult for you to accept love and kindness from others?

Action Step:

Perform an act of self-love today, something that makes you feel cared for and appreciated. Additionally, allow yourself to accept a gesture of kindness from someone else without deflecting or minimising it.

Today's Notes:

Write about the act of self-love you chose and how it made you feel. Also, note your experience with accepting kindness from others and any feelings it brought up.

Words of Wisdom:

Day 9: Today, embrace the love and kindness that you deserve. Remember, you are absolutely worthy of gentleness from yourself and warmth from others.

Day 9 Girl Power Notes

Your very own space for notes!

Day 10

Affirmation: "My voice is valuable, and my contributions matter."

Today's Focus:

Acknowledging the value of your voice and contributions is vital for building confidence and self-esteem. This affirmation is a reminder that what you have to say is important, and your actions have an impact. It encourages you to speak up and participate actively in areas that matter to you.

Reflection Question:

Can you recall a time when you hesitated to express your opinion or thought your contribution wasn't important? How might things have been different if you had recognised the value of your voice?

Action Step:

Today, make it a point to share your thoughts in a discussion or offer your help in a situation where you normally wouldn't. Observe how it feels to assert the value of your voice and contributions.

Today's Notes:

Reflect on your experience of sharing your thoughts or contributing. How did it affect your self-perception and the way others engaged with you?

Words of Wisdom:

Day 10: Today, let yourself be heard! Speak your truth with confidence that your words and ideas are not only valid but invaluable! Be your own catalyst for change.

Day 10 Girl Power Notes

Your very own space for notes!

Day 11

Affirmation: "I find joy in the present moment."

Today's Focus:

Living in the present is a powerful practice for enhancing one's quality of life. This affirmation encourages mindfulness and appreciation of life's simple pleasures. By finding joy in the present moment, one cultivates a sense of contentment and reduces stress.

Reflection Question:

How often do you find yourself preoccupied with past events or worried about the future? What's one simple pleasure that brings you joy in the present moment?

Action Step:

Dedicate a few minutes today to engage fully with a simple activity that brings you joy, whether it's savouring a cup of coffee, listening to a favourite song, or feeling the sun on your skin. Focus entirely on the experience.

Today's Notes:

Describe the activity you chose and how it made you feel to be fully present. Did you notice any details that you usually overlook?

Words of Wisdom:

Day 11: Take joy in the present moment; it's where life unfolds and where you truly live. Today, let every second be a celebration, a chance to savour the here and now, enriching your life with the fullness of simply being.

Day 11 Girl Power Notes

Your very own space for notes!

Day 12

Affirmation: "I grow stronger with every challenge I face."

Today's Focus:

This affirmation builds on the understanding that challenges are not just obstacles but opportunities to become stronger and more resilient. It's a reminder that your strength grows not despite difficulties but because of them.

Reflection Question:

Think about a challenge that made you stronger. How did facing and overcoming that challenge contribute to your resilience?

Action Step:

Consider a current challenge in your life. Identify a strength you've gained or can gain from this experience. Take one small step today that demonstrates your strength in this area.

Today's Notes:

Reflect on the challenge and the strength you identified. How does recognising your growth change your approach to current and future challenges?

Words of Wisdom:

Day 12: As you face today's challenges, remember to trust in your resilience - You Got This!

Day 12 Girl Power Notes

Your very own space for notes!

Day 13

Affirmation: "I trust my intuition and make wise decisions."

Today's Focus:

This affirmation emphasises the power of trusting your own instincts and making decisions that align with your true self. It's about acknowledging your inner wisdom and feeling confident in the choices you make based on that insight.

Reflection Question:

Recall a time when you listened to your intuition, and it led you to a positive outcome. How did it feel to trust yourself in that moment?

Action Step:

Today, trust your intuition when making a decision. Before deciding, take a moment to quiet your mind and listen to what your gut is telling you. Then, follow through based on this inner guidance.

Today's Notes:

Reflect on the decision you made using your intuition. How did the process and outcome compare to times when you've made decisions purely based on logic or advice from others?

Words of Wisdom:

Day 13: Trust the wisdom of your inner voice today, its the compass that will guide you to wise decisions. Believe in your intuition; its a powerful ally on your journey!

Day 13 Girl Power Notes

Your very own space for notes!

Day 14

Affirmation: "I am open to new experiences and embrace learning."

Today's Focus:

Being open to new experiences enriches your life and fosters personal growth. This affirmation encourages you to step out of your comfort zone, be curious, and embrace the learning that comes from new adventures.

Reflection Question:

Is there something new you've been wanting to try but have hesitated? What has held you back?

Action Step:

Identify one new experience you can introduce into your life this week. It could be trying a new hobby, reading a book outside your usual genre, or even exploring a new place.

Today's Notes:

Write about the new experience you chose and what you learned from it. How did it feel to open yourself up to something new?

Words of Wisdom:

Day 14: Open the door to new experiences and let curiosity be your guide. Each new step is a chance to learn and grow.

Day 14 Girl Power Notes

Your very own space for notes!

Day 15

Affirmation: "I release what no longer serves me."

Today's Focus:

This affirmation focuses on the liberating act of letting go—whether it's negative thoughts, toxic relationships, or outdated self-beliefs. Releasing what no longer serves you creates space for new growth and possibilities.

Reflection Question:

What are you holding onto that's no longer serving your well-being or growth?

Action Step:

Choose one thing you're ready to release. It could be an item, a grudge, or a self-limiting belief. Acknowledge it, thank it for its role in your life, and then let it go.

Today's Notes:

Reflect on the process of letting go. How did it make you feel? Do you feel lighter or more open to the future?

Words of Wisdom:

Day 15: Letting go free's you up for the future. Release what doesn't serve you and watch your path clear for new possibilities.

Day 15 Girl Power Notes

Your very own space for notes!

Day 16

Affirmation: "My happiness is a reflection of my inner peace."

Today's Focus:

Happiness that comes from within is not dependent on external circumstances. This affirmation reminds us that true contentment and joy originate from a place of inner peace and self-acceptance.

Reflection Question:

What practices or habits contribute to your sense of inner peace and, consequently, your happiness?

Action Step:

Engage in an activity today that promotes your inner peace; this could be meditation, a nature walk, or simply sitting quietly for a few moments of reflection.

Today's Notes:

Note the activity you chose and its effect on your mood and overall sense of well-being. How can you incorporate more of this into your daily routine?

Words of Wisdom:

Day 16: Find your happiness from within today. Nurture your inner peace and let it be the source of your joy.

Day 16 Girl Power Notes

Your very own space for notes!

Day 17

Affirmation: "I am resilient, strong, and capable of overcoming anything."

Today's Focus:

This affirmation is about recognising your strength and resilience in the face of adversity. It's a declaration of your ability to overcome challenges and emerge stronger on the other side.

Reflection Question:

Think of a challenge you overcame in the past. What strengths did you discover in yourself through that experience?

Action Step:

Identify a current challenge and affirm your strength and resilience in addressing it. Write down three strengths you possess that will help you overcome this obstacle.

Today's Notes:

Reflect on the affirmation of your resilience and strengths. How does this perspective shift your approach to the challenge?

Words of Wisdom:

Day 17: Remember, you are the embodiment of strength and resilience, face today's challenges with the knowledge that you are capable of overcoming anything.

Day 17 Girl Power Notes

Your very own space for notes!

Day 18

Affirmation: "I am deserving of success and abundance."

Today's Focus:

This affirmation aims to boost your self-worth and attract success and abundance into your life. It's about believing in your deservingness of all things good and working towards them with confidence.

Reflection Question:

Have you ever felt undeserving of success or abundance? What beliefs might be driving those feelings?

Action Step:

Visualise yourself achieving a goal that symbolises success or abundance to you. Then, take one small step today that moves you closer to that vision.

Today's Notes:

Write about your visualisation and the steps you took towards it. How does affirming your deservingness affect your motivation and actions?

Words of Wisdom:

Day 18: You are deserving of success and abundance in all its forms. Step into this belief and see where it takes you.

Day 18 Girl Power Notes

Your very own space for notes!

Day 19

Affirmation: "I nurture my body with love and respect."

Today's Focus:

This affirmation highlights the importance of treating your body with care, love, and respect. It's about recognising your body's needs and responding to them with kindness and nurturing.

Reflection Question:

Reflect on how you currently care for your body. Are there ways you might be neglecting its needs or treating it harshly through your words or actions?

Action Step:

Commit to one act of physical self-care today that feels nurturing and respectful. This could be as simple as enjoying a nutritious meal, taking a leisurely walk, practising yoga, or ensuring you get enough rest.

Today's Notes:

Document the act of self-care you chose and how it made you feel. Consider how incorporating regular, mindful self-care can impact your overall well-being and self-esteem.

Words of Wisdom:

Day 19: Cherish your body like the treasure it is. Nourish it with love and respect; it will. be your steadfast companion.

Day 19 Girl Power Notes

Your very own space for notes!

Day 20

Affirmation: "I cultivate gratitude for the abundance in my life."

Today's Focus:

Cultivating gratitude shifts your focus from what's lacking to the abundance already present in your life. This affirmation encourages you to recognise and appreciate the wealth of blessings around you, fostering a sense of contentment and joy.

Reflection Question:

What are three things you're grateful for today? How does focusing on these aspects of your life change your mood or outlook?

Action Step:

Start a gratitude journal, if you haven't already. Each morning or evening, write down three things you're grateful for. Make this practice a regular part of your day to continually cultivate gratitude.

Today's Notes:

After writing in your gratitude journal, reflect on the experience. How does acknowledging your blessings influence your perception of abundance in your life?

Words of Wisdom:

Day 20: Gratitude turns what we have into enough and more! Today, let thankfulness fill your heart and draw abundance into your life.

Day 20 Girl Power Notes

Your very own space for notes!

Day 21

Affirmation: "I find strength in vulnerability."

Today's Focus:

Embracing vulnerability is a sign of strength, not weakness. This affirmation encourages you to see vulnerability as an opportunity for growth and connection, allowing yourself to be open and authentic with others and yourself.

Reflection Question:

Can you think of a moment when being vulnerable led to a deeper connection or personal growth? How did that experience change your view of vulnerability?

Action Step:

Reach out to someone you trust and share something personal you've been keeping to yourself. Observe how this act of vulnerability feels and the outcome it brings.

Today's Notes:

Reflect on your experience with vulnerability today. What did you learn about yourself and the power of opening up?

Words of Wisdom:

Day 21: Embrace vulnerability as your hidden strength; let it forge deeper connections and reveal your authentic self.

Day 21 Girl Power Notes

Your very own space for notes!

Day 22

Affirmation: "I choose to see the good in others."

Today's Focus:

Looking for the good in others can transform your relationships and bring more positivity into your life. This affirmation is about adopting a compassionate, positive outlook that seeks to understand and appreciate others' qualities.

Reflection Question:

Think of a recent challenging interaction. How might seeing the good in the other person change your perspective on the interaction?

Action Step:

Today, make a conscious effort to identify and mentally acknowledge something positive about everyone you interact with, no matter how small.

Today's Notes:

Note your observations and feelings about focusing on the positive traits of others. How did this approach affect your interactions and mood?

Words of Wisdom:

Day 22: Seeing the good in others reflects the goodness within you. Today, let this perspective brighten your interactions.

Day 22 Girl Power Notes

Your very own space for notes!

Day 23

Affirmation: "I embrace my journey, knowing each step moves me forward."

Today's Focus:

You are recognising that every experience, whether perceived as positive or negative, contributes to your journey and growth. This affirmation encourages patience and trust in your path, knowing that each step has value.

Reflection Question:

Reflect on a past event you initially viewed as a setback. In hindsight, how did it contribute to your growth or move you forward?

Action Step:

Identify an area of your life where you've felt stuck or impatient. Reaffirm your commitment to your journey and take one small action step that represents progress in this area.

Today's Notes:

Write about the action you took and how it symbolises trust in your journey. How does it feel to acknowledge every step as progress?

Words of Wisdom:

Day 23: Every step on your journey counts! Embrace each one, knowing you're moving forward, close to where you want to be.

Day 23 Girl Power Notes

Your very own space for notes!

Day 24

Affirmation: "I am a creator of peace in my life and in the world."

Today's Focus:

This affirmation highlights your role in fostering peace, both internally and externally. It's about choosing actions and thoughts that promote harmony and understanding, starting with yourself and radiating outward.

Reflection Question:

What are some ways you can create more peace in your daily life? How can your actions contribute to peace in your broader community or the world?

Action Step:

Engage in a peaceful activity today, such as meditating, performing a random act of kindness, or resolving a minor conflict. Notice the impact of this action on your sense of peace and the atmosphere around you.

Today's Notes:

Reflect on your experience with creating peace. How did the activity affect your inner peace and the environment or relationships involved?

Words of Wisdom:

Day 24: Create peace in your world and let it ripple out. Your presence can turn the tide towards harmony.

Day 24 Girl Power Notes

.Your very own space for notes!

Day 25

Affirmation: "My creativity and uniqueness are my superpowers."

Today's Focus:

Celebrating your unique creative abilities and the innovative perspectives you bring to the world. This affirmation is a reminder that your creativity is a powerful asset and an expression of your individuality.

Reflection Question:

How do you express your creativity? In what ways does your uniqueness shine through in your life and work?

Action Step:

Dedicate time today to a creative endeavour that brings you joy, or try something new that sparks your creativity. Embrace the process without judgement.

Today's Notes:

Write about the creative activity you chose and how it made you feel.

How does honouring your creativity and uniqueness impact your self-esteem and confidence?

Words of Wisdom:

Day 25: Your creativity and uniqueness are your gifts to the world. Unleash them and watch how they transform your life.

Day 25 Girl Power Notes

Your very own space for notes!

Day 26

Affirmation: "I let go of comparisons and embrace my own path."

Today's Focus:

This affirmation addresses the destructive habit of comparing ourselves to others. It encourages you to focus on your journey, recognising that everyone's path is different and valuable in its own way.

Reflection Question:

Think of a recent instance when you compared yourself to someone else. How did it make you feel, and how might things be different if you focused on your path instead?

Action Step:

Whenever you catch yourself comparing today, redirect your focus to one thing you appreciate about your journey. Write it down if possible.

Today's Notes:

Reflect on your experiences with letting go of comparisons. How does focusing on your path change your feelings about yourself and your journey?

Words of Wisdom:

Day 26: Step away from the shadows of comparison. Your path is yours alone, brilliant and incomparable.

Day 26 Girl Power Notes

Your very own space for notes!

Day 27

Affirmation: "I am patient with myself and trust in the timing of my life."

Today's Focus:

Cultivating patience can be transformative, allowing you to take life at your own pace and trust in the unfolding of your journey. This affirmation encourages agentle, trusting approach to personal growth and life's challenges, acknowledging that everything comes in its own time.

Reflection Question:

Recall a time when something didn't happen on your timeline, but the timing was perfect in hindsight. How does this perspective shift your current view on patience and timing?

Action Step:

Identify an area of your life where you've felt impatient or pressured. Commit to releasing that urgency today. Instead, do something symbolising trust in the process—like planting a seed, literally or metaphorically.

Today's Notes:

Reflect on the act of trusting in timing and how it feels to release urgency. What insights do you gain about patience and trust in your life's timing?

Words of Wisdom:

Day 27: Practice patience with yourself and trust the timing of your life. Great things are taking shape, even if they're not yet visible.

Day 27 Girl Power Notes

Your very own space for notes!

Day 28

Affirmation: "I give and receive love freely and joyfully."

Today's Focus:

This affirmation emphasises the flow of love as a natural, enriching part of life. It's about opening your heart to give love without reservation and receive love without barriers, enriching your connections with joy and warmth.

Reflection Question:

Think about how you express love. Are there barriers that prevent you from giving or receiving love fully? What steps can you take to open your heart more?

Action Step:

Make an intentional effort to express love in a way you normally wouldn't, whether it's through words, a gesture, or an act of kindness. Be equally open to receiving expressions of love from others.

Today's Notes:

Write about your experiences of giving and receiving love today. How did these actions make you feel? Did you notice any changes in your relationships or in yourself?

Words of Wisdom:

Day 28: Love is a two-way street of giving and receiving. Today, travel this road with an open heart and open arms.

Day 28 Girl Power Notes

Your very own space for notes!

Day 29

Affirmation: "I acknowledge my achievements and celebrate my growth."

Today's Focus:

Recognising and celebrating your achievements, no matter how small reinforces a positive self-image and motivates further growth. This affirmation is a reminder to honour your progress and the effort it took to get where you are today.

Reflection Question:

Reflect on the past month. What achievements, learning experiences, or moments of growth stand out to you? How often do you take the time to celebrate these victories?

Action Step:

Choose one achievement or area of growth from the past month and celebrate it in a meaningful way. This could be treating yourself, sharing your accomplishments with others, or simply taking a moment to feel proud.

Today's Notes:

Document the achievement you celebrated and how you honoured it. Reflect on how celebrating your growth impacts your view of yourself and your journey.

Words of Wisdom:

Day 29: Celebrate your victory, small and large, for they all contribute to the magnificent journey you are on.

Day 29 Girl Power Notes

Your very own space for notes!

Day 30

Affirmation: "I am on a continuous journey of self-discovery and improvement."

Today's Focus:

As you conclude this 30-day challenge, this affirmation serves as a reminder that personal growth and self-discovery are ongoing processes. It's an invitation to keep exploring, learning, and evolving with curiosity and openness.

Reflection Question:

Looking back over the past 30 days, what have you discovered about yourself? How do you plan to continue on your path of self-discovery and improvement?

Action Step:

Set a new goal or intention based on your reflections and learnings from this challenge. Outline the first few steps you'll take to pursue this goal, ensuring it aligns with your continued journey of self-improvement.

Today's Notes:

Reflect on the entire 30-day experience. Note the affirmations that resonated most, the insights gained, and how you've grown. Consider how you'll incorporate these affirmations and lessons into your daily life moving forward.

Words of Wisdom:

Day 30: As this challenge concludes, remember that self-discovery is an unending adventure. Keep exploring, keep growing and keep shining!

Day 30 Girl Power Notes

Your very own space for notes!

Well done, and Congratulations!

Well done on your incredible 30-day journey with "Empower Your Mind: 30 Days of Affirmations for Women," your Girl Power has shone through as you have made a brilliant commitment every day with your Affirmations.

Each day, with every affirmation spoken, you've woven a tapestry of confidence and self-love that is as unique as it is beautiful.

Reflect upon the moments of discovery, the quiet introspection, the breakthroughs, and even the challenges. Each was a step on a path that you navigated with grace and determination.

Think back to Day 1, remember the intentions you set, and look at yourself now; you've grown in ways only this journey could reveal.

What insights shone brightest for you? Which affirmations felt like keys unlocking parts of yourself that were waiting to be freed? Hold these close; they are your treasures to keep.

You've shown up for yourself in the most powerful way possible, and we hope you carry forward this energy and self-belief into every facet of your life. You are a testament to the unyielding power of a woman who dares to embark on the quest for self-empowerment and self-discovery.

From all of us at Girl Power Rocks, we salute you, we thank you, and we invite you to continue this incredible journey. May the seeds of positivity you've planted blossom into a garden of endless possibility.

With heart-felt congratulations,

Estelle Mutum,

Founder of Girl Power Rocks

What Next?

Thank you so much for taking the time to read and work through this book.

It has been a pleasure sharing it with you. If you are seeking women's empowerment as part of your self-discovery and personal growth journey, please feel free to join us at Girl Power Rocks.

https://www.instagram.com/girlpowerrocks_world/

https://www.facebook.com/groups/girlpowerrockscommunity

www.girlpowerrocks.com

GIRL
POWER
ROCKS

Resources

Hay, L. L. (2009). *You can heal your life.*

Peale, Norman Vincent. The power of positive thinking. New York: Prentice-Hall, Inc. 1952. 276 P. $2.95. (1955). *Science Education, 39*(1), 68. https://doi.org/10.1002/sce.3730390129

Handy, R. T. (1964). Spirits in Rebellion: The Rise and Development of New Thought. By Charles S. Braden. Dallas: Southern Methodist University Press, 1963. xii, 571 pp. $7.50. *Church History, 33*(2), 226–227. https://doi.org/10.2307/3162993

Helmstetter, S. (2017). *What to say when you talk to your self.* Simon and Schuster.

Creswell, J. D., Dutcher, J. M., Klein, W. M., Harris, P. R., & Levine, J. M. (2013). Self-affirmation improves problem-solving under stress. PLOS ONE, 8(5), e62593.

Cohen, G. L., & Sherman, D. K. (2014). The psychology of change: Self-affirmation and social psychological intervention. Annual Review of Psychology, 65, 333-371.

About the Author

Estelle Mutum, founder of Girl Power Rocks and a certified Women's Coach and member of the International Coaching Federation (ICF) Estelle, specialises in Women's Empowerment Coaching and has created Girl Power Rocks Ltd to support women on their journey of self-discovery, personal growth, and limitless potential. Come join us, and let's work together to shape a world where you are the master of your own destiny. Your Girl Power starts with YOU!

You can connect with me on:

https://girlpowerrocks.com

https://www.facebook.com/groups/girlpowerrockscommunity

Printed in Great Britain
by Amazon

41227304R00066